FAULT LINES

UNDERSTANDING THE POWER OF EARTHQUAKES

Johanna Wagstaffe

ORCA BOOK PUBLISH

Library and Archives Canada Cataloguing in Publication

Wagstaffe, Johanna, author
Fault lines : understanding the power of earthquakes
/ Johanna Wagstaffe.

Includes bibliographical references and index.

Issued in print and electronic formats.
ISBN 978-1-4598-1243-7 (hardcover).—ISBN 978-1-4598-1244-4 (pdf).—
ISBN 978-1-4598-1245-1 (epub)

1. Earthquakes—Juvenile literature. I. Title.
QE534.3.W34 2017   j551.22   c2017-900850-1
c2017-900851-x

First published in the United States, 2017
Library of Congress Control Number: 2017933023

Summary: This fully illustrated, nonfiction book for middle readers focuses on earthquakes, how they happen and what you need to know.

Orca Book Publishers is dedicated to preserving the environment and has printed this book on Forest Stewardship Council® certified paper.

Orca Book Publishers gratefully acknowledges the support for its publishing programs provided by the following agencies: the Government of Canada through the Canada Book Fund and the Canada Council for the Arts, and the Province of British Columbia through the BC Arts Council and the Book Publishing Tax Credit.

Edited by Merrie-Ellen Wilcox
Design by Jenn Playford
Front cover art by Shutterstock.com
Back cover art from left to right: iStock.com, iStock.com, Dreamstime.com, Alamy Stock Photo

ORCA BOOK PUBLISHERS
www.orcabook.com

Printed and bound in Canada.

20 19 18 17 • 4 3 2 1

Background graphic: JUANLJONES/ISTOCK.COM

To my parents.

*And to Tristan, who will always wake me up
when there is an earthquake.*

Table of Contents

Introduction

Showing off my school uniform on my first day of kindergarten in Tokyo. My little sister, Jessica, is in the stroller beside me.
PIROSKA WAGSTAFFE

WHEN I WAS FOUR YEARS OLD, I lived with my family in Tokyo, Japan. I remember seeing the polite nods and warm smiles in the crowded subways, riding on the back of my mother's bicycle through the alleys of the city, and wishing we could visit the five-story Sanrio toy store. I also remember the regular *earthquake* drills in our kindergarten class. We would scramble to get under the desks and then line up and march outside. It seemed like a fun game at the time, but there was seriousness about it.

I first felt the ground move one day when I was playing at home after school. I had cleared out a bookshelf to use as a Barbie house—when suddenly all the toy furniture started shaking and falling off the shelf. I did what we had practiced at school and crawled under the coffee table, calling out to my parents. It was only a small quake, but the strangeness of the feeling of having no control stuck with me, as did the sense of how well prepared the Japanese were. Maybe that was what led me to study earthquakes later on.

Back in Canada, when I got to high school, *geography* (the study of the earth's surface) made perfect sense to me. The earth's processes explained things that we could see around us. The water cycle explained why it rained. The force of flowing water on a bank carved out the curves of a river. But there are still mysteries, and scientists are still learning how our planet works.

At university, I wanted to understand more about how our world worked, so I took *seismology* (the study of earthquakes)—and got completely hooked on the earth. After four years of learning what happens under our feet, I wanted to learn more about what happens above our heads, so I went to another university to learn about *meteorology* (the study of the atmosphere, including climate and weather).

When major earthquakes happen around the world, part of my job as a journalist is to explain to our viewers the science of what is happening. Here, I am reporting on a large earthquake that struck off the coast of Japan in November 2016. CBC

Along with covering breaking news, I also do in-depth science stories. Here, I am interviewing the assistant fire chief for Vancouver Fire and Rescue Services about the kinds of drills the city practices in preparation for a major earthquake. JESSICA LINZEY

From the movement of the tectonic plates under our feet to the shifting weather systems above our head, our planet is always in motion. NASA

The fields of meteorology and seismology are not all that different. In both, scientists observe our planet's processes and apply what we've learned in the past to make conclusions about what's going to happen in the future. In meteorology we study current conditions like temperature, pressure and cloud cover to figure out how they are going to change in a few days. In seismology we study the waves that earthquakes send out to understand the stresses that are building up below us, and what areas might be at risk for earthquakes in the future. And as you'll see, in my job as a *meteorologist* and science reporter I get to do both: explain the weather every day, and explain earthquakes whenever there is a major one somewhere on earth.

In *Fault Lines: Understanding the Power of Earthquakes*, I'm going to tell you a little bit about what goes on beneath our feet, and how we can prepare for earthquakes, wherever we happen to live. You'll see that *seismologists* are like detectives, examining data from earthquakes to understand what's going on inside our planet. It's not nearly as quiet down there as you might think!

Whether it's creating forecasts, tracking storms or analyzing the data after an earthquake, my days as a science reporter are never dull! CBC

Here's what the International Space Station looks like orbiting Earth. Those astronauts probably have the ultimate view of how our planet's natural processes fit into place!

GOLKIN ANDREY/
DREAMSTIME.COM

A Planet in Motion

Johanna's Story

During my years at university, I discovered that I liked getting other people excited about science, and finding easy and interesting ways to explain the science of the world we live in. After university I found my ideal job, working behind the scenes at the Canadian Broadcasting Corporation (CBC) as a meteorologist, helping to forecast Canada's weather. Eventually I got to come in early in the morning to try presenting forecasts live on TV.

A few months later, there was news of an earthquake in Los Angeles. It happened during the day, and we were getting a lot of pictures of the shaking and how scared people were. The *magnitude* 5.5 earthquake struck only 45 kilometers (28 miles) east of downtown Los Angeles and damaged buildings in the area.

During the Los Angeles earthquake, I moved from the green screen, where I presented the weather, to the anchor desk, where we discussed what I knew about the breaking news event. KELLY DOHERTY

I realized I could add a lot of important information to the news we were reporting. I was able to explain to viewers how strong the earthquake was, how widely it was felt and if there was a possibility of *aftershocks*. I explained that Los Angeles is located in an area where earthquakes of that size are quite common and don't usually mean a larger one is coming.

Luckily, that earthquake wasn't very strong, and there were no injuries. But it made me realize that understanding more about what's going on during a natural disaster like an earthquake can be useful and even comforting, especially for people who have family and friends there. It can also get people talking about how to prepare for future earthquakes where they live.

No lives were lost due to the 2008 Chino Hills earthquake near Los Angeles, but it did cause significant structural damage throughout the area.
JASON SHERWIN/WIKIPEDIA.ORG

ANGRY GODS

The earliest earthquake that we have a written record of was in China in 1177 BCE, more than 3,000 years ago. There are many other accounts of large earthquakes that have happened around the world since then. In the past, people who felt the ground moving under their feet often believed that it was the result of angry gods or mystical creatures.

Scientists began recording and locating earthquakes in the early 19th century but it wasn't until the 1930s that seismologists discovered that the earth has an inner core. This quickly led to a better understanding of what causes earthquakes. With many questions still to be answered, seismology is a very exciting field to be in.

In a way, seismologists are the ultimate detectives, examining data from earthquakes past and present to understand what's going on inside our planet. Even when there are no human records, seismologists are able to study ancient earthquakes and *tsunamis* by examining clues from the past—in tree rings, core samples (small samples of earth drilled from below the surface) and evidence of ancient tsunamis. Many scientists believe that the processes that create earthquakes today probably began over a billion years ago.

ON THE MOVE

To understand how earthquakes happen, we first have to understand how the inside of our planet works.

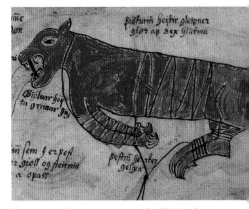

A seventeenth-century manuscript illustration of the river monster Fenrir. In Norse mythology it was said that this giant wolf's jaw could shake the earth. ANDREZC/WIKIMEDIA COMMONS

QUAKE FACTS

Shallow earthquakes—those that happen between the surface and 70 kilometers (43 miles) below the surface—are often more destructive than deep earthquakes. The less rock that the seismic waves have to travel through, the less energy is diffused before they reach the surface. And that can mean more powerful shaking.

QUAKE FACTS

About 90 percent of all earthquakes and 75 percent of all volcanoes happen in what is known as the Ring of Fire, a 40,000-kilometer (25,000-mile) horseshoe that stretches from the southern tip of South America, along the coast of North America, across the Bering Strait between Alaska and Russia, down through Japan and into New Zealand. It is actually where the tectonic plate under the Pacific Ocean, the Pacific Plate, bumps and grinds against all the surrounding plates.

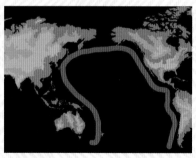

The Ring of Fire is a major area that surrounds the Pacific Ocean in which a large number of earthquakes and volcanic eruptions occur. FARSAD-BEHZAD GHAFARIAN/DREAMSTIME.COM

The earth consists of many layers, which are constantly in motion. And it all begins in the scorching center—the *core*. In fact, the core has two layers: the inner core is solid, and the outer core is liquid. Both layers are made up mainly of iron and some nickel, at temperatures over 5,000 degrees Celsius (over 9,000 degrees Fahrenheit)!

The outer core is spinning around the solid inner core, and this motion radiates heat toward the next layer—the *mantle*. Heated *magma* rises from the mantle, travels to the earth's outer layer—the *crust*—cools and sinks back down, only to be heated up in the core again. This process, called *convection*, makes the surface of the planet shift continually.

The earth's crust is actually a thin, rocky shell that is divided into small pieces that all fit together, a bit like a cracked eggshell. The pieces are called *tectonic plates*, and the cracks are called *faults*. But not all faults are on plate boundaries, because sometimes there are faults and earthquakes within one tectonic plate. The San Andreas fault is an example of a fault that is also a plate boundary because there is a different tectonic plate on either side of the crack. As the crust shifts, because of the convection below, the tectonic plates bump, slide and grind past each other. Most of the time, the plates are moving only about as fast as your fingernails grow—so even though the ground you're standing on is moving all the time, the movement isn't noticeable at all.

Tectonic plates interact with each other on the surface of the earth in three different ways. They move toward each other, move away from each other or slide past each other.

BUMP!

Two plates moving toward each other and colliding form what is called a *convergent boundary*. This is where some of the world's tallest mountains are created and where most volcanoes form. It's also where the world's biggest earthquakes occur. But what happens at convergent boundaries depends on what kinds of plates are crashing into one another.

The active Bromo volcano in East Java, Indonesia, was formed by the collision of two tectonic plates.
NOPPAKUN/DREAMSTIME.COM

The earth is not just one big solid ball throughout. There are actually four main layers. Some are liquid, some are solid, and some are in between! JENN PLAYFORD

Layers of the Earth

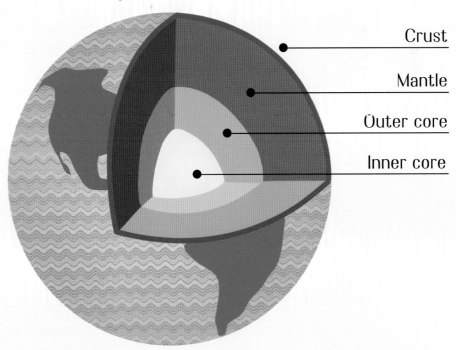

Crust

Mantle

Outer core

Inner core

Here an old fault line is clearly visible as a deep crack on the surface of the earth in Utah, a reminder of the incredible stresses that are taking place under our feet.
LINDA BAIR/
DREAMSTIME.COM

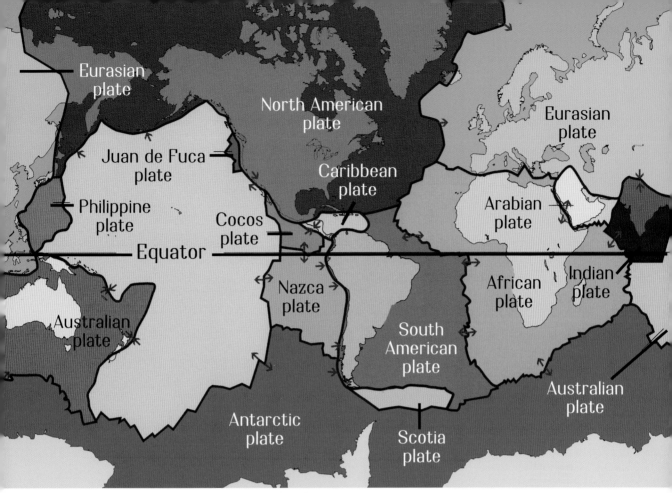

Eurasian plate

North American plate

Eurasian plate

Juan de Fuca plate

Caribbean plate

Arabian plate

Philippine plate

Cocos plate

Equator

African plate

Indian plate

Nazca plate

Australian plate

South American plate

Australian plate

Antarctic plate

Scotia plate

Earth's outer shell is divided into several plates that glide over the mantle. As these plates interact with each other, earthquakes can occur. USGS/WIKIPEDIA.COM

If two continental plates—like the ones that make up most of the planet's land masses—are pushing into each other, it's called a *continental collision*. The two plates crumple and fold into each other, often forming great mountain chains because the ground has nowhere to go but up. For example, the Eurasian and Indian Plates have been pushing into each other for tens of millions of years, and the Himalayas continue to grow by about 6 centimeters (2.4 inches) a year. So don't wait too long if you are planning to climb Mount Everest!

Damaged airplanes in Sendai, Japan float in the water left by a massive tsunami after a magnitude 9.0 earthquake struck just the day before.

THE ASAHI SHIMBUN/ GETTY IMAGES

If an oceanic plate is colliding with a continental plate, it's a different story. This is called a *subduction zone*. Because the rock that makes up the oceanic plates is colder and denser, it sinks and slides under the hotter and lighter rock of the continental plate. When the cold top layer of the oceanic plate, the *oceanic crust*, hits the planet's hot mantle layer, it begins to melt. The melted sections of oceanic crust then rise through the continental plate, forming new continental crust as well as mountains and even volcanoes. As one plate tries to slide past the other, though, sections of them can get stuck, eventually causing earthquakes.

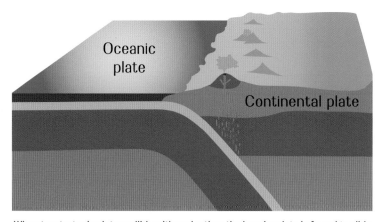

When two tectonic plates collide with each other, the heavier plate is forced to slide below the lighter plate. This subduction zone is where much of the action on the earth occurs, including earthquakes and volcanoes. JENN PLAYFORD

This is the only situation where earthquakes greater than magnitude 9.0 can happen. There are subduction zones off the coast of southern British Columbia, where I live. In fact, most countries that border the Pacific Ocean have a subduction zone just off their coast.

M9.0: BRITISH COLUMBIA, 1700

Those of us living in British Columbia often hear about the "big one"—the *megathrust* earthquake that will happen one day off the west coast of Vancouver Island, where the part of Juan de Fuca plate that is being forced under the North American plate will suddenly snap back. Scientists believe that the last time this happened was in 1700. Core samples from the ocean floor provide evidence of this. Tree rings along the Pacific North-west coast indicate a major tsunami along the coast.

First Nations historical accounts suggest the tsunami destroyed entire villages on Vancouver Island. And there are records of a massive tsunami around that time in Japan. Megathrust earthquakes don't stick to an exact schedule, but we do know that stress has been building up in the Cascadia Subduction Zone for about 300 years. While the odds of it happening today are relatively small, there is a 10 percent chance that it will happen within the next fifty years. And it is almost certain that it will happen sometime in the next few hundred years.

QUAKE FACTS

Earthquakes last only a few seconds or minutes. But the process that leads to the release of stress deep within the planet involves many different steps and lasts much longer than the shaking we feel on the surface.

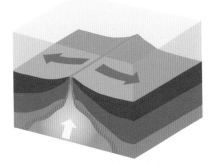

A divergent boundary is formed when two tectonic plates are moving away from each other, allowing magma from deep in the earth to well to the surface.
JENN PLAYFORD

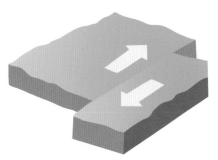

When two tectonic plates slide past each other, they create a transform boundary often transforming what the surface of the earth looks like.
JENN PLAYFORD

SPLIT!

Two plates moving away from each other form a *divergent boundary*. Most of the active divergent boundaries today occur between two ocean plates, so they are often located in the middle of an ocean. As the plates move apart, magma from deep within the earth oozes up through the gap between the two plates. When it hits the cold water, it hardens into solid rock, forming brand-new crust.

One of the most famous divergent boundary settings is the Mid-Atlantic Ridge, which runs along the floor of the Atlantic Ocean all the way up through Iceland. In fact, the whole island of Iceland was created over millions of years by *lava* (magma that breaks through the earth's surface) rising and piling up, layer after layer.

SLIDE!

Two plates sliding past each other create a *transform boundary*. As sections of these kinds of faults try to slide past each other, they get stuck, causing earthquakes. No land is being created or destroyed in this case, but over several million years, huge areas of land that were once side by side can end up hundreds of kilometers away from each other. It's sort of like a two-lane highway where each lane is actually moving in the opposite direction.

The most famous transform boundary is the San Andreas Fault, which runs right through California.

Iceland sits on the boundary between two tectonic plates that are pulling apart, so magma often bubbles to the surface. These lava fountains were 100 meters (328 feet) high in the area of Iceland that saw eruptions in 2014.
JUEMIC / DREAMSTIME.COM

Q&A

Q: HOW MANY EARTHQUAKES HAPPEN AROUND THE WORLD EVERY YEAR?

A: Scientists believe that millions of earthquakes occur each year on our planet. But most are either too small to be felt or detected, or they happen in unpopulated areas of the world where no one feels them. About one million earthquakes are actually recorded around the world each year. Of those, only about 100,000 can actually be felt, only 100 or so cause damage, and a very small number actually result in deaths.

Earthquakes often happen in California—as the two plates grind against each other. Since San Francisco and Los Angeles sit on opposite sides of the fault, in a few million years the two cities could be right beside each other.

There is also a transform boundary off the coast of central and northern British Columbia, called the Queen Charlotte Fault. And there's a transform boundary that runs almost the entire length of New Zealand's South Island.

A STRESSFUL SITUATION

So how exactly are earthquakes triggered? It all comes down to stress.

As two plates try to move past one another (either side by side or on top of each other), things don't always

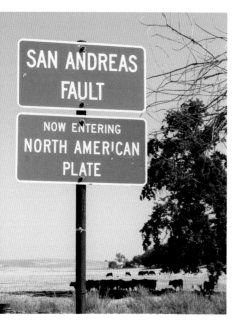

Cattle graze on the infamous San Andreas Fault line in Parkfield, CA. Parkfield is the most closely observed earthquake zone in the world because it sits right on top of the line. EHUGHES/ISTOCK.COM

go smoothly. Sometimes the two plates can become completely stuck and stop moving. But as the rest of the plates continue to move, the pressure builds up in the stuck section. Even though the plates are only moving centimeters per year, a lot of pressure builds up over several decades to a few hundred years. Eventually the stress becomes too great, and all that stored-up energy is suddenly released all at once—as an earthquake. The section of the earth that actually moves and releases stress during an earthquake is known as the *rupture zone.*

Once the energy has been released, the plates can slide past each other again, until the next time they get stuck and the stress builds again.

A crack in the hills after an earthquake in New Zealand. Earthquakes can change the landscape of cities and countries in a single moment. HASLINDA /DREAMSTIME.COM

M9.5: CHILE, 1960

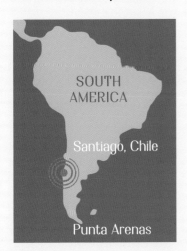

On May 22, 1960, the largest earthquake ever recorded struck southern Chile, where the Nazca Plate is trying to slide underneath the South American Plate. The magnitude 9.5 earthquake was shallow, at just 33 kilometers (20 miles) below the surface. The shaking lasted for ten minutes. It also produced deadly foreshocks and aftershocks, a killer tsunami and even a volcanic eruption. Four foreshocks leading up to the earthquake, including a magnitude 7.3 the day before, caused extensive damage. Each of them also transferred stress onto the stuck section of the fault, which led to the megathrust earthquake.

This monster earthquake actually ruptured almost 1,000 kilometers (620 miles) of rock and moved it about 50 meters (164 feet). The sudden release of stress snapped the seafloor upward by 6 meters (20 feet) and dropped the coastline by about 3 meters (10 feet), resulting in a massive tsunami that swept across the Pacific Ocean, killing many people in Japan and the Philippines. Over 1,600 people were killed in Chile, and millions were left homeless. Aftershocks continued for years, some as large as magnitude 7.0.

M6.9: AUSTRALIA, 1968

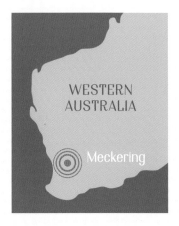

WESTERN AUSTRALIA

Meckering

On October 14, 1968, a 40-second earthquake of magnitude 6.9 destroyed the town of Meckering, Australia. Many buildings in Perth, 130 kilometers (80 miles) away, were also damaged. Amazingly, no one was killed, but many were injured. Western Australia isn't near any major tectonic boundary, but the continent is colliding with the Pacific Plate to the east and the Eurasian Plate to the north. So even though much of Australia is far away from these collision zones, there is still a lot of stress building up inside the plate. This makes Australia different from most other earthquake zones.

RIDING THE WAVES

The exact point at which all that energy is released within the earth during an earthquake is called the *hypocenter*. The **epicenter** is the point on the earth's surface directly above the hypocenter.

When energy is released from the hypocenter, it is sent out in all directions as *seismic waves*. There are many different kinds of seismic waves. The shaking that we feel during an earthquake is actually one of the last types of waves to reach the earth's surface.

The first wave to reach the surface is the **primary wave**, or **P wave**. P waves can travel through both solid rock and liquids like water or the more fluid layers of the earth. And they can travel up to twenty times faster than a jet! Most of the time, though, we can't really feel P waves.

The next wave to arrive on the surface is called the *secondary wave*, or *S wave*. S waves can only move through solid rock. They can't travel through the liquid outer core of the earth or bodies of water like the oceans and lakes.

P waves and S waves are called *body waves* because they travel through the body of the earth. The next waves to arrive during an earthquake are called **surface waves**. They travel along the earth's surface, shaking the ground either side to side or in a rolling motion like ocean waves. It is the S waves and the surface waves that cause most of the damage in an earthquake.

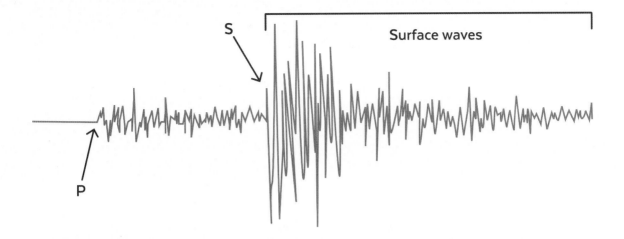

This is a typical earthquake signal. By measuring the time difference between the arrival of the P and S waves and performing some calculations, it is possible to determine where the earthquake happened. JENN PLAYFORD

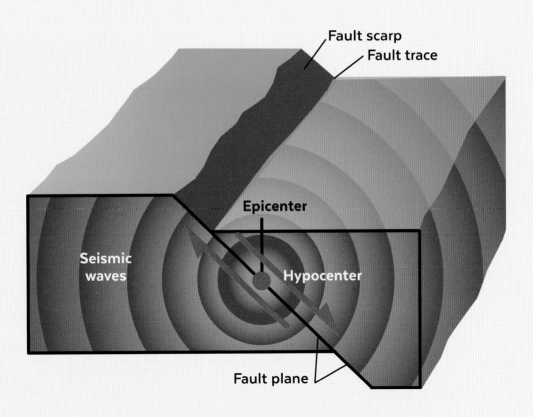

The hypocenter is the exact point where the earthquake begins. If you draw
a line straight up to the earth's surface from the hypocenter, that is the epicenter. JENN PLAYFORD

My grandparents and my mother as a little girl, shortly after they arrived in the Australian outback as refugees from Hungary. JENO KORA

ONE EVENING NOT LONG AGO, I was having dinner with my family. I was telling them about my research for this book when my grandmother said, "It was very scary for me when I experienced the big earthquake in Australia." We all stopped eating and turned to look at my grandmother. My grandparents and their young daughter, Piroska (my mother), had fled Hungary during the revolution in 1956. We knew about their terrifying nighttime escape across the Danube River, and about their living in refugee camps in the former Yugoslavia for almost a year before being chosen to board a boat bound for Australia to start a new life in the outback. But we didn't know about the magnitude 6.9 earthquake that struck almost directly under their small town in Western Australia, near Meckering, almost destroying it completely. We asked my grandmother to tell us more.

Eszter Kora, AUSTRALIA

It happened on a public holiday. I remember because Papa and little Irene and George were all home for the day. But Piroska (who was fourteen at the time) had signed up for a walkathon with the school and had just left for her friend's house, where they would catch the school bus together. Not long afterward, it started to pour. I jumped in the car to take some rain gear to the friend's house down the street. But I was too late—they had already left on the school bus.

As I stood just inside the doorway of the friend's house, wondering if I should chase them down, the floor under me started to shake. Things started falling off the walls and countertops. I yelled to the family in the house that we were having an earthquake and to get outside! But they just stood there, stunned. I ran out to the verandah. At that point the shaking was so violent I couldn't even walk properly. I didn't know where to put my feet. I looked around and the beams on the porch started to buckle, and I was scared they were going to come down. I ran out into the middle of the street and noticed that some of the hydro wires were starting to snap. I was scared that they were going to electrocute me.

Finally the shaking stopped. All I could think about was my family. I drove back home as fast as I could, getting more and more upset as I noticed the damage to the buildings on the street. Some had even collapsed.

My mother (Piroska) and my Mama and Papa in the back with my Uncle George and Auntie Irene in the front. This is right around the time that the earthquake happened. JENO KORA

Papa, Irene and George were okay though. Papa said that it was very scary. The shaking was so strong it shook the fridge out into the middle of the kitchen floor.

I had to find Piroska. I had never felt more scared in my whole life, because I didn't know where she was or if she was okay. I spent the rest of the day driving around through the desert, trying to find my daughter. The radio stations had started reporting all the damage to the town. They said that one of the roads had been ripped open. I was so scared that Piroska had fallen into one of those holes. I didn't find her until the school bus returned them at the end of the day, and I have never felt so much relief. When I asked her about the earthquake, she said that she felt the ground buckle underneath her—but at that point they had been walking in the hot sun in the open desert for a few kilometers, and she thought maybe she was just feeling a little faint from exertion!

The next day we all drove to look at the tear in the road. It was 3 meters (10 feet) deep and almost 40 kilometers (25 miles) long. It took a long time for the town to recover, and as a result they upgraded the *building codes* in Australia to withstand earthquakes better. I still have nightmares about that day—not knowing if my whole family was okay for so long.

Learning about seismic upgrading and earthquake engineering from the director of the Earthquake Engineering Research Facility at the University of British Columbia, Vancouver, BC. JESSICA LINZEY

Magnitudes and Epicenters

Johanna's Story

Weather can often impact people who are already experiencing traumatic situations, like earthquakes. Part of my job is figuring out if weather will make a situation better or worse.
CLIFF SHIM

I was at work on January 12, 2010, the day a magnitude 7.0 earthquake struck Haiti. I provided what information I could about the science of the earthquake. It was a fairly big earthquake, so many aftershocks would likely follow. And it was a shallow quake—only 13 kilometers (8 miles) deep. With less distance for the waves to travel, the shaking would have been felt strongly. Information trickled slowly out of Haiti, because damaged power lines had cut off communication with much of the country. But we eventually learned that about 3.5 million people experienced intense shaking, which caused heavy damage to buildings and poorly constructed homes.

As a meteorologist, I knew that with more than a million people now living on the street or in shantytowns

with no running water and no sanitation, the earth-quake and continued aftershocks were the least of their problems. Thunderstorms were common, even in the winter months, and the makeshift shelters that so many people were living in couldn't stand up to strong winds and heavy rain. Many of Haiti's forests had been cut down in the past, and without trees holding the soil in place, heavy rains could easily trigger landslides and flooding. And the muddy camps made it easier for disease to spread. The poor weather also made it hard for aid workers to get to the hardest-hit areas. And this was supposed to be the dry season.

Recovery efforts were still under way in August 2012, when Tropical Storm Isaac hit Haiti. Severe flooding caused more deaths. In October that year, an even stronger storm, Hurricane Sandy, hit the country, leaving large parts of it underwater and killing more people. Even today, every time a new tropical storm forms in the Caribbean, I watch the forecasts to see if Haiti is in the possible line of the storm.

Survivors sift through clothing donations after the Haiti earthquake.
JOE PASSARETTI/CBC

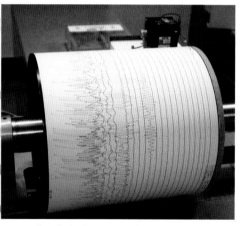

QUAKE FACTS

For most earthquakes, the Richter estimates are roughly the same as the moment magnitude estimates. But only the moment magnitude scale can measure an earthquake greater than magnitude 8.0.

A typical seismometer drum recorder used to detect and record earthquakes before recent digital upgrades. Z22/WIKIPEDIA.ORG

A GIANT PEN

Think about what happens when you throw a stone in a pond. The ripples move out in all directions from the point where the stone hit the water. The same thing happens when there is an earthquake, with the waves radiating away from the hypocenter, right through the earth. By studying the different seismic waves that an earthquake sends out, scientists can learn a lot about the quake.

Detectors called *seismometers* have been set up all over the world to pick up seismic waves traveling through the earth. They can tell us exactly where an earthquake happened and how strong it was. Seismometers are so sensitive that they can detect even the smallest earthquake—or large earthquakes very far away.

So how do they work? A seismometer is basically a weight hanging from a supporting structure that is anchored to the ground. When the ground shakes, the anchor moves, but the hanging weight stays still and records the ground moving around it. It's kind of like holding a pen in one place over a piece of paper and then moving the paper around beneath it to draw a picture. In this case, the picture is the movement of the earth, and it's called a *seismogram*. This is what seismologists read to get information about an earthquake.

MEASURING MAGNITUDE

In 1934 a seismologist called Charles F. Richter developed a tool to measure medium-sized earthquakes in California. The *Richter scale* became one of the first widely used methods of measuring the magnitude of earthquakes. It used a formula based on the largest wave recorded on a seismometer and the distance between the earthquake and the seismometer.

Seismometer on the slope of the Klyuchevskoy volcano in Russia. The volcano is active, so detecting earthquakes in the area can be a sign of an impending eruption.
AASK/DREAMSTIME.COM

Children in Haiti stand on what's left of a building after the 2010 earthquake. JOE PASSARETTI/CBC

M7.0: HAITI, 2010

On January 12, 2010, a magnitude 7.0 earthquake struck 25 kilometers (15 miles) west of Haiti's capital, Port-au-Prince. Haiti sits just where the Caribbean Plate meets the North American Plate, and the Caribbean Plate is sliding past the North American Plate by about 20 millimeters (less than an inch) per year. An estimated three million people were affected by the quake, with between 100,000 and 300,000 killed. As many as 250,000 homes and other buildings were severely damaged. Construction standards are low in Haiti. There are no building codes, and often structures and homes are just built wherever they fit. Many hospitals, airports, seaports and communication systems were also damaged by the earthquake, which made it difficult for people from other countries to get supplies and help to those in need. Cholera and other disease outbreaks continue to plague the survivors. At least fifty-two aftershocks measuring magnitude 4.5 or greater have been recorded. Haiti continues to deal with the impacts of the earthquake today.

Although people became very familiar with this scale, it doesn't work well with large earthquakes. Today, scientists prefer the *moment magnitude scale*, which works for a wider range of earthquake sizes. Introduced in 1979, the scale determines the size of an earthquake based on how much energy is released. It's the actual distance that a fault moved, and the force required to move it that far.

The Canadian Disaster Assistance Response Team arrives in Nepal after the 2015 earthquake. SAŠA PETRICIC/CBC

For most of the measurements that we do every day, we use a linear scale, where each amount on the scale has increased by the same amount over the previous amount—as on a ruler. Earthquake magnitudes are based on a *logarithmic scale*, where each whole number you go up on the scale is the previous amount multiplied by

Volunteers work to clear the rubble following the 2010 Haiti earthquake. JOE PASSARETTI/CBC

QUAKE FACTS

People often wonder if there is such a thing as an "earthquake season" or "earthquake weather." As far as scientists know, there is no such thing, and the time of the year does not affect the occurrence of earthquakes.

The classic mushroom-cloud shape of a nuclear explosion. Imagine that kind of energy being released under your feet during a large earthquake!
WITOLD KRASOWSKI/DREAMSTIME.COM

another amount. For example, a magnitude 5.0 earthquake would result in ten times more shaking than a magnitude 4.0 earthquake, and thirty-two times as much energy would be released.

The reason for using a logarithmic scale to measure earthquakes is that earthquakes come in an extremely wide variety of sizes—ranging from a tremor that can't be felt on the earth's surface to earthquakes that destroy entire cities. (And the moment magnitude scale also has no upper limit, so it can describe earthquakes of unimaginable and inexperienced intensity.) If we used a linear scale to measure earthquakes, we would have to use giant numbers to describe the earthquake size. For example, a magnitude 9.0 earthquake releases one trillion times more energy than a magnitude 1.0!

THAT'S A LOT OF ENERGY!

We can think about the energy released in earthquakes like the energy released in explosives. A magnitude 6.0 earthquake releases the equivalent of about 15 kilotons of *TNT*. That's similar to the atomic bomb dropped on Hiroshima during World War II. A magnitude 13.0 earthquake would be about equal to the energy released when an asteroid or comet smashed into Mexico sixty-five million years ago and helped to wipe out the dinosaurs.

So far, the largest earthquake ever recorded by seismologists was a magnitude 9.5 in Chile in 1960. That's 20,000 times larger than the atomic bomb that was dropped on Hiroshima in 1945.

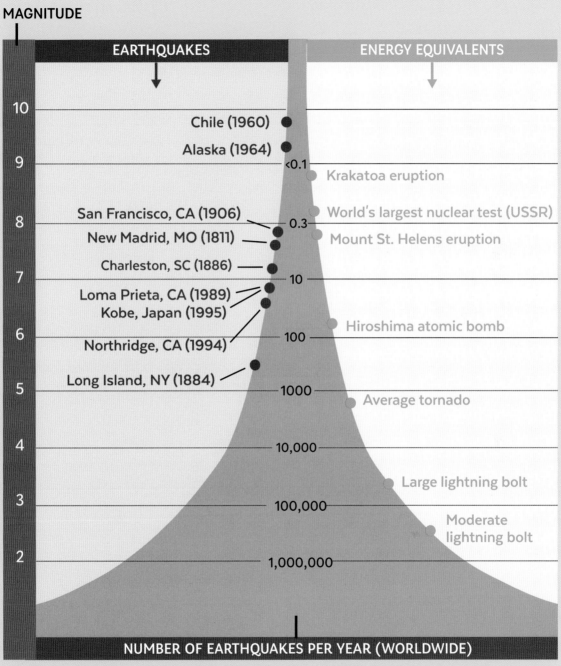

A comparison of historical earthquakes and the kind of energy that was released. JENN PLAYFORD

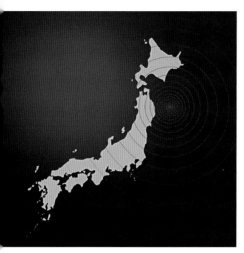

The epicenter of the 2011 Japan earthquake. Locating the epicenter as quickly as possible can help determine where the hardest-hit areas might be. CHUONGY/DREAMSTIME.COM

LOCATING EPICENTERS

Seismologists determine the epicenter of an earthquake by looking at the information from at least three different seismometers. Since P waves travel faster than S waves, the P waves arrive at a seismometer first. The first wiggly lines on a seismogram represent the arrival of the P waves. The S waves will be the second, larger set of wiggly lines. The surface waves arrive last, and they are the largest of the three and the most spread out.

First, using the seismograms from each of the different seismometers, seismologists measure the

Q & A

Q: DO OTHER PLANETS HAVE QUAKES?

A: Yes! The shaking and rolling motions that we experience here on Earth happen on other planets, moons and even stars. But not all galactic quakes are created equal.

Most planets and moons that are made up primarily of rock, like Earth, started off with a molten core as well. Sometimes astronomers can see signs of volcanic activity on the surface, which means there has been activity beneath the surface at some point— and that means quakes. In the 1960s and 1970s, the Apollo astronauts placed seismometers on the surface of the moon, and many moonquakes were detected—some as strong as magnitude 5.0. It turns out that the gravitational force from Earth is one of the causes of quakes on the moon.

Other bodies in our solar system, like the sun, get seismic activity from other forces, like pressures from different gases. Some "starquakes" in far-off galaxies are so big that they can be seen through telescopes.

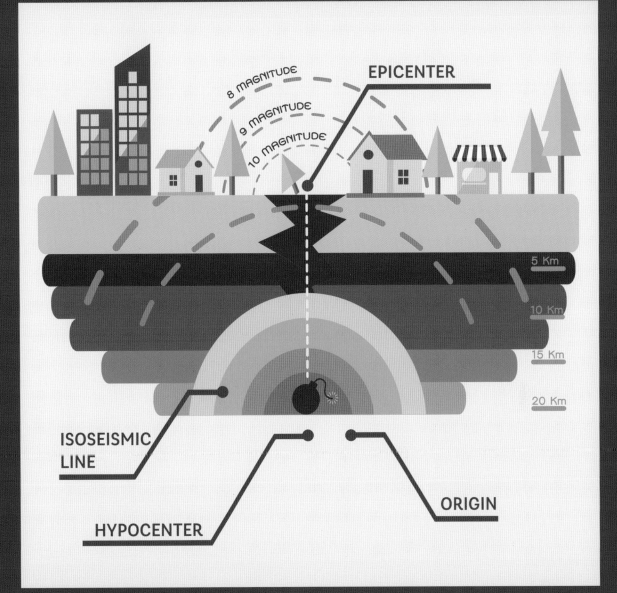

The energy released by an earthquake radiates out from the hypocenter in all directions. Generally, the closer you are to the epicenter, the stronger the shaking. RAFTEL/SHUTTERSTOCK.COM

Over 120,000 homes were damaged beyond repair in the magnitude 7.6 earthquake that struck northwestern Turkey in 1999. SADIK GÜLEÇ/ DREAMSTIME.COM

time between the P waves and the S waves to determine the distance of the epicenter from each station. Since P waves travel faster than S waves, the closer you are to an earthquake, the closer together the P waves and S waves will be. (Think of a thunderstorm: the less time that passes between the lightning and the thunder, the closer you are to the storm. It's the same with the P waves and S waves of an earthquake.)

Then they draw a circle representing the distance of the epicenter from each station. Where the circles intersect is the epicenter.

It used to be a big job to figure all that out, picking out the P waves and S waves in the seismogram and calculating distances. But today, computer programs can do this automatically, providing an initial estimate of magnitude and location within seconds of an earthquake.

Rescue teams search for earthquake victims with the help of dogs after an earthquake in 2011 in Van, Turkey.
SENGULMURAT/ISTOCK.COM

M7.6: TURKEY, 1999

On August 17, 1999, a magnitude 7.6 earthquake struck just 11 kilometers (6.8 miles) southeast of the city of Izmit, Turkey. The country sits on the Anatolian Plate, but is surrounded by three other huge plates—Eurasian, African and Arabian—which are all moving toward each other. As a result, Turkey gets pushed westward along two main fault lines. It was along the northern transform fault that a 150-kilometer (93-mile) section of the plate ruptured westward about 5.7 meters (18 feet), just 17 kilometers (10 miles) below the surface. Strong shaking lasted for thirty-seven seconds. More than 17,000 people were killed, nearly 50,000 were injured, and half a million people were left homeless.

The 1999 earthquake was just one in a string of deadly earthquakes in Turkey as stress was passed down the locked segments of the fault. A magnitude 7.2 struck just a few months later, followed by a magnitude 6.4 in 2003 and a magnitude 6.0 in 2010. This pattern of earthquakes suggests that Istanbul is at risk for a large earthquake at some point in the future.

Ten-year old Esra Söylemez in her school uniform. After the earthquake in 1999, her school had many earthquake drills in case another one hit. BETUL SÖYLEMEZ

Esra Söylemez
TURKEY

When I was ten years old, the biggest earthquake in Turkish history struck an area called Gölcük, which is roughly halfway between Istanbul and the capital, Ankara. It had a magnitude of 7.6, with aftershocks of 4.0 to 5.0.

I was in bed when it happened and didn't feel anything. When my mother woke me and told me to change my clothes, I thought we were just going for a nighttime picnic. My father had already gone outside and was shouting at me and my brother to hurry up. There we joined our neighbors and some friends. Everyone was really afraid.

There was no phone service, so we couldn't contact my grandparents, who were also affected in Ankara.

Everyone slept outside in the woods for the next three or four days, except my fifteen-year-old brother. He's always been the brave one in the family! One night my best friend came and stayed with us in the woods. I remember we had chocolate and chips, which was fun. Luckily, it was summer and the weather was nice.

Eventually people started leaving the woods and returning to their homes. When I went back to school a few days later, everyone was sharing their experiences. Teachers carried out drills to prepare us in case another quake struck.

I thought I wasn't affected by what happened, but I was. I couldn't sleep properly for about a year afterward and had terrible dreams almost every night. I was so scared, I would sleep in my parents' bed, as I was feeling phantom aftershocks.

With so many damaged homes after the 1999 Turkey earthquake, thousands of people had to stay in makeshift shelters on the streets. The fear of aftershocks kept people outside for weeks. SADIK GÜLEÇ/SHUTTERSTOCK.COM

3

More Than Just Shaking

Johanna's Story

The 2011 Japan earthquake is the fourth-most-powerful earthquake in the world since modern record-keeping began. Even to this day, there are new studies and updates to report on about the science and impact of the event. CBC

When the magnitude 9.0 earthquake happened in Japan on March 11, 2011, I was living in Toronto. My dad called me very early in the morning, so I knew right away that something was wrong. He told me a large earthquake had struck Japan and to turn on the TV—the monster tsunami that was washing ashore was being broadcast live around the world. We were silent on the phone together as we watched in disbelief. The wave was slowly and destructively pushing inland—taking with it boats, cars, planes and eventually homes and other buildings. You could even see people in the water.

It was the largest earthquake to hit Japan in modern times and the fourth most powerful in the world since record-keeping began in 1900. But the

world knew before all the numbers came out that it was a major catastrophe.

I wasn't supposed to be working that day, but I went to the studio right away. In the days that followed, I explained what had happened and why the tsunami was so bad. I explained the continuing aftershocks—and eventually what we knew about how much the ground had actually moved.

But the quake had caused another disaster: the resulting tsunami had damaged the Fukushima Daiichi nuclear reactors. Radiation was leaking from the reactors, and hundreds of thousands of people in nearby towns were being evacuated. It was a very dangerous time in Japan. And I was supposed to be flying to Tokyo three weeks later. I had booked a solo trip to finally visit the country I grew up in as a little girl. But now I didn't even know if my flight would still be running. (More about that in chapter 4.)

Sendai Airport after the tsunami from the 2011 earthquake off the coast of Japan. Not only were the tarmac and runways submerged but water reached up to the second level of the passenger terminal as well. U.S. AIR FORCE PHOTO/ WIKIPEDIA.ORG

A cracked road after the magnitude 7.8 earthquake that struck Ecuador in 2016. Many strong aftershocks followed, making recovery efforts even more difficult. FOTOS593/ SHUTTERSTOCK.COM

Having the ground shaking violently beneath you is already a challenge. But earthquakes can cause lots of other problems as well.

FORESHOCKS AND AFTERSHOCKS

Smaller earthquakes sometimes happen before the main quake is triggered. These are called foreshocks. Imagine that you are trying to open a door that has become jammed shut. As you pull on the door handle, you may feel the door begin to move toward you a little bit. But it's not until the door flies open, sending you flying backward, that the pressure has fully been released. Those initial, but smaller, movements of the door are similar to foreshocks.

It would be great if we could tell when an earthquake is a foreshock, because then we would know that a larger earthquake is coming. Since foreshocks often happen just a day or two before the main quake, people would have time to get to a safe area. But not all earthquakes have foreshocks, so we will likely never know if an earthquake is the main quake in a sequence or if it's actually a sign of something larger to come.

More common than foreshocks are aftershocks. These are smaller earthquakes that happen after the main quake, and they represent the earth settling into its new position. But they are all earthquakes in their own right, and sometimes they can be just as scary and damaging as the main quake. Aftershocks can happen for days, weeks, months and even years after the main earthquake.

A tsunami warning sign in Japan, telling people to get to higher ground if they feel an earthquake. WINHORSE/ISTOCK.COM

QUAKE FACTS

A tsunami is actually a series of ocean waves. Sometimes the time between waves can be longer than ten minutes. If the trough, the section between the tops of the waves, arrives at the shoreline first, it can pull back the water close to shore, revealing seafloor that is usually underwater. This is called drawback, and it's one of the warning signs that a large wave is coming. Sometimes people who don't know what's happening are curious to see the exposed shore and run out to take a look.

Generally, though, they get smaller and less frequent over time.

Aftershocks also tell us how much of the earth actually moved as stress was released. Sometimes the area that has moved in an earthquake is a rectangle hundreds of kilometers long, but just a few meters wide. This is the rupture zone, and all of the aftershocks will happen within it.

WALLS OF WATER

When an earthquake happens under an ocean, the energy that is released at the epicenter can actually move the ocean floor. Movement of the ocean floor in turn displaces the water above it, forming a tsunami wave. As the tsunami wave continues to travel away

As a tsunami moves into more-shallow water, the wave is forced to grow in height as it approaches land. JENN PLAYFORD

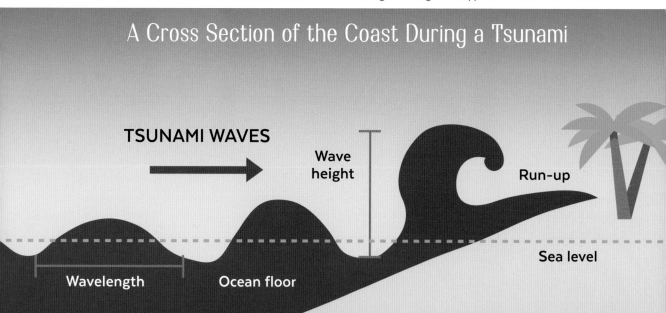

A Cross Section of the Coast During a Tsunami

TSUNAMI WAVES

Wave height

Run-up

Sea level

Wavelength

Ocean floor

from the epicenter and toward coastlines, where the water is shallower, the wave is forced to slow down, which compresses it and makes it higher—sometimes several meters high. The wall of water can move inland, destroying coastal communities that lie in its path.

Traveling as fast as jetliners, tsunamis can arrive on the opposite coastlines of the ocean a few hours after an earthquake happens hundreds of kilometers away. Luckily, warning systems around the world are getting better and better at calculating if and where a tsunami might hit after an earthquake. Most coastal communities on the Pacific Ocean now have tsunami evacuation warning sirens and routes that will get people to higher ground quickly. But smaller or remote communities that may not have instant access to phones, alerts or sirens are still at risk.

Even though tsunami waves can travel as fast as a jet, they still take hours to cross oceans. Here is an example of a tsunami forecast, showing how many hours after an earthquake in Chile it will take for the first waves to reach various points in the Pacific Ocean. JENN PLAYFORD

M9.0: JAPAN, 2011

On March 11, 2011, a section of the Pacific Plate, which is sliding under the continental plate that Japan lies on, ruptured. The resulting magnitude 9.0 earthquake triggered a tsunami that swept across the Pacific Ocean and leveled entire towns and villages on the coast of northern Japan. The tsunami reached as high as 38 meters (125 feet) and traveled inland as far as 10 kilometers (6 miles). Almost 16,000 people were killed. The tsunami caused a nuclear meltdown at the Fukushima Daiichi Nuclear Power Plant. Japan's total economic loss was more than $300 billion. Radiation continues to leak from the damaged reactors, and many people will never be able to return to the area. The massive amount of debris from the tsunami's destruction continues to wash up on coastlines on the other side of the Pacific Ocean, thousands of kilometers away.

A girl stands in front of a giant ship that was swept inland by a tsunami. This picture was taken one year and eleven months after the 2011 Tohoku earthquake and tsunami in Japan, but you can still find evidence of the disaster today. ARTWAYPICS/ISTOCK.COM

WALLS OF EARTH

Earthquakes can also trigger landslides, mudslides and avalanches. Or these are triggered by aftershocks when the initial earthquake has loosened the soil or snow. Many high-risk earthquake zones are located near mountains, because of all the geologic activity below. The shaking from an earthquake can loosen rock, mud or even an entire hillside, and the wave of debris can wipe out whole villages in the valleys or on the slopes.

Landslides also make it hard for rescue workers to reach these areas, because there is often only a single road that leads into the village. If that gets cut off or washed out by a landslide, helicopters are the only way in.

An entire street collapsed in Anchorage, AK, following a large earthquake in 1964.
LIBRARY.USGS.GOV/WIKIPEDIA.ORG

M8.0: MEXICO, 1985

On September 19, 1985, a magnitude 8.0 earthquake struck just off the west coast of Mexico, where the Cocos Plate is pushing against and sliding under the North American Plate. The shaking lasted for more than five minutes in some areas. The worst damage was in Mexico City—more than 350 kilometers (215 miles) away. Why did Mexico City, so far away, get the worst of it? The main reason is geology. The downtown area of Mexico City was once an island in the middle of a lake. The lake was eventually drained, and the city continued to expand outward. As a result, most of the city is built on an old lake bed made up of soft clay with high water content. The shaking from the earthquake resulted in liquefaction. The lake bed also resonated with certain seismic waves and actually increased the effect of the shaking. Over 400 buildings collapsed, and another 3,100 were seriously damaged. The earthquake caused at least 5,000 deaths, many the result of collapsing buildings.

The front end of a van is swallowed up by the ground as a result of soil liquefaction caused by the 2011 earthquake near Christchurch, New Zealand. MARTIN LUFF/ WIKIPEDIA.ORG

LIQUEFACTION

Sometimes the shaking of the ground during an earthquake is made worse by the type of soil that a city is built on. One of the most dangerous things that can happen during an earthquake is a phenomenon called *liquefaction*. If soil is sandy or silty, water can fill the gaps between the grains. During the shaking, the water pressure between the grains of sand builds up, and the contact between each grain is lost. Once-solid ground suddenly acts more like Jell-O.

Soil Liquefaction

STABLE SOIL
Building stands erect on stable soil.

LIQUEFIED SOIL
Shaking and tilting causes some structures to fail. Building tilts and sinks as soil stability declines.

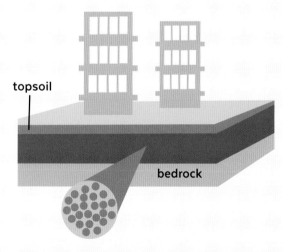

Loosely packed grains of soil are held together by friction. Pore spaces are filled with water.

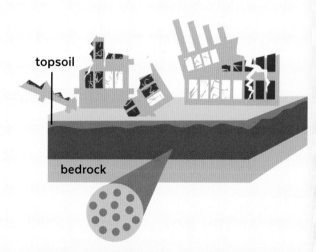

Shaking destabilizes the soil by increasing the space between grains. With its structure lost, the soil flows like a liquid.

When you walk along a beach near the water, water is pushed out by your foot when you step down, and you leave a footprint in the sand behind you. But if you tap your foot repeatedly on the surface of the sand, you create a soggy, muddy area.

Now imagine what happens if buildings are sitting on top of this kind of soil during an earthquake. The shaking is much greater—like shaking a bowl of Jell-O. Liquefaction has toppled buildings this way in many great earthquakes.

The 2011 Christchurch earthquake forced thousands of tons of liquefied sand and mud up to the surface through cracks and craters in the roads. In some areas streets were covered for months. NIGEL SPIERS /DREAMSTIME.COM

Q & A

Q: CAN ONE EARTHQUAKE TRIGGER ANOTHER?

A: Sometimes after a large earthquake, earthquakes around the world seem to increase in frequency. One reason for this is that we are paying more attention to earthquakes after a big one.

In fact, hundreds of quakes occur every day—many that are large enough for people to feel on the ground. And even though an earthquake sends seismic waves reverberating through the earth, like a ringing bell, it is not likely to trigger another large earthquake on the other side of the world. Most places where stress has been building up for years on a fault line will just go when they are ready to go. The seismic waves from a faraway earthquake might add to those stresses, but the second earthquake was likely very close to happening anyway.

It is a different story, though, when it comes to earthquakes happening on the same fault line. If several sections of a fault line are stuck and waiting to release stress, they may end up connecting during a big earthquake. Hundreds of kilometers (miles) of fault can rupture at once—kind of like unzipping a zipper. That's what happened in Japan in 2011.

FLOODS AND FIRES

Rescue crews head out in the flooded streets of Japan after the 2011 tsunami to search for survivors.
CHIEFHIRA/WIKIMEDIA.ORG

Sometimes earthquakes can actually break dams or levees along rivers, leading to major flooding that can wash away buildings. Tsunamis may also cause flooding in coastal areas.

In addition, earthquakes can start dangerous fires, especially in cities. In the past, the shaking would start fires by knocking over things like candles, lanterns and woodstoves. Today, it may rupture gas lines or topple power lines. And with cars and debris blocking the streets, and the pipes that supply water damaged by the shaking as well, it may be hard for emergency crews to fight the fires.

Here sandbags were placed to protect against flooding after a tsunami in Same Beach, Ecuador.
FOTOS593/SHUTTERSTOCK.COM

The ground level of a building gives way after the Loma Prieta earthquake in California. The side-to-side motions of an earthquake can collapse base levels if they are not built to earthquake code. J.K. NAKATA/USGS.GOV

COLLAPSING BUILDINGS

Sometimes when a large earthquake hits a major city, there is minimal damage. But in other cases, a smaller earthquake completely destroys an entire area. Often, the difference comes down to the way the buildings are constructed.

The greatest earthquake damage commonly happens in very dense cities, where buildings may be poorly constructed. Unfortunately, the cheapest and easiest structures to build are sometimes the deadliest during an earthquake. Buildings designed to house a lot of people above shops on the ground floor frequently have fewer stabilizing walls, because the commercial space below is left open for the shops or for parking. During the shaking, then, the ground floor collapses first.

QUAKE FACTS

Most injuries and deaths from earthquakes, especially in countries with building codes that address earthquake safety, are caused not by collapsing buildings but by falling objects. People are much more likely to be injured or killed by a light fixture or a heavy piece of furniture than by a building collapsing. A natural reaction when the shaking starts might be to run outside, but that is where you are most at risk of having objects fall on you.

Sometimes seismic upgrades can make an existing building earthquake resistant. Here, external bracing is added to a concrete parking garage in California. LEONARD G./WIKIPEDIA.ORG

Buildings that are made of stone and mortar also tend to collapse easily during a quake. That is why old buildings in cities and towns, as well as buildings in rural areas of many countries, are often the hardest hit.

There are ways to strengthen poorly designed buildings, but they may be too costly for cities in poorer countries. In countries like Japan, the United States and Canada, however, many older buildings are being "retrofitted" to meet newer standards for earthquake safety. It is expensive, though, and earthquake-prone cities like Vancouver and San Francisco are still working on it.

Engineers and seismologists can work together to determine what kind of structures will be safest during

M7.8: SAN FRANCISCO, 1906

On April 18, 1906, a magnitude 7.8 earthquake struck the coast of Northern California. "The Great Earthquake" ruptured a 476-kilometer (296-mile) section of the San Andreas Fault, the boundary between the Pacific Plate and the North American Plate. In some places along the fault, the ground split open, leaving crevices as large as 6 meters (20 feet) wide. The epicenter was very close to San Francisco, which led to violent shaking for 45 to 60 seconds. A fire broke out in the city and lasted for several days, killing 3,000 people and destroying over 80 percent of San Francisco. Geologists at the time couldn't understand what had caused the massive movement of the ground, but their research resulted in a major breakthrough in understanding how energy is spread during an earthquake—science that is still used today.

an earthquake. Building codes in many places require new buildings to be earthquake-safe. But even these aren't perfect. Most modern building codes require that a building "stay standing" during an earthquake, but that doesn't mean it will be good enough to live in afterward.

When a magnitude 6.3 earthquake struck Christchurch, New Zealand, in 2011, only a handful of buildings collapsed. Since then, however, over 1,200 buildings have had to be demolished—most of the city's downtown—because they were no longer safe to live in. Imagine surviving an earthquake and then having nowhere to live. This is one of the major issues facing cities in earthquake zones today.

Rebuilding the city of Christchurch, New Zealand. Over 10,000 houses required demolition after the 2011 earthquake. CHAMELEONSEYE/SHUTTERSTOCK.COM

As damaging as the earthquake and aftershocks were in San Francisco in 1906, the fires that burned out of control afterward were even more destructive. CHADWICK, H.D./WIKIPEDIA.ORG

Ria, JAPAN

We were in school when the shaking started. Lots of things fell off the walls, including a big TV. I was scared, but we always have drills at school, so we knew what to do right away. We got under our desks and waited there for the shaking to stop. Then the teacher led us all outside to wait for our families to come and get us. My dad eventually came to get my sister and me, but we kept feeling the ground shake from the aftershocks, and it was still scary. We knew we were safe from tsunamis where we were, but some of my friends were worried.

When we got back to our house, the inside was a mess. I was most worried about my pet rabbit, Dumbo, but he was hiding under the stairs, so he was okay. It was really hard to get water because ours wasn't working. And we could only buy food that had been tested to make sure it was safe from radiation—even our school lunches.

Ria holding her beloved pet rabbit, Dumbo, who hid under the stairs during the Japan earthquake.
SEAN MAHONEY

Eventually we went to Canada to our cousins' house, where we were safer. When we came back to Japan, we stayed at our grandparents' home. They live on top of a mountain, so they didn't get as much damage from the earthquake.

Now we always keep extra water in the house in case we have another earthquake. And when we have drills in school, they remind us how scary the earthquake was and why it's important to practice.

Hiroko, JAPAN

I had my backpack on my desk because we were just getting ready to leave school for the day. At first the shaking wasn't that big, but then I had to hold on to my desk because the whole desk was shaking from side to side, not just my body. That was the first time I had felt shaking that strong. It was scary. Lots of kids were crying and worried about where their families were. There was a big fish tank in our classroom, and it fell over and shattered. (At least there were no fish in it at the time.)

My dad came and picked my sister and me up after about an hour. But my mom is a teacher at our school, so she had to stay for four hours to evacuate all of the children.

It was really hard after the earthquake, because we had no water. Even when we cooked we couldn't wash the frying pan with water, so we had to put aluminum foil on the pan and then throw the foil out afterward.

Now when the earthquakes come, I'm not as scared, because I know we've had our big one.

Hiroko enjoying a huge apple. After the earthquake it was very hard to cook and wash, as there was no running water for days. SEAN MAHONEY

4

On the Ground and in the Sky

Johanna's Story

Mr. Hiroshi showing me around Kyoto just a few weeks after the 2011 earthquake. I made lifelong friends during that trip even though it was such a difficult time for the country.
JOHANNA WAGSTAFFE

had always wanted to return to the place where I lived as a child, and where so many of my first memories are from. When the 2011 earthquake happened, my trip to Japan had been booked for months, and I was supposed to leave in three weeks. With radiation leaking from the damaged Fukushima nuclear plant, I knew I might have to cancel the trip. I spoke to reporters who had already gone and come back to see what they thought about safety. The radiation had not yet affected Tokyo. I created a backup plan and bought a one-way train ticket south in case the radiation situation got worse. My dad bought me iodine pills—a potentially life-saving measure in case I was exposed to radiation. The day before the flight, I decided it was safe enough to go.

I was nervous when I landed in Tokyo. There were no tourists on the streets. People were going about their daily lives, but something felt wrong. The flashing lights of the famous Shibuya Crossing had been turned off in order to save electricity, since power was being diverted to the region that was affected by the nuclear disaster. There was obvious damage to some buildings, and the trains were being shut down after every aftershock. The tourist attractions were closed, and the few people I spoke to seemed very somber. I wondered if I should have come at all.

After a day in Tokyo, I took a train south to Kyoto. As I wandered about the beautiful temples and shrines of Japan's former imperial capital, I felt sad that I was unable to really help after such a tragedy. I was sitting on a rock, thinking and taking in the scenery, when an elderly Japanese man sat down beside me. We started talking, and he kindly offered to take me around the city. He was practicing a tour that he was going to give to visiting students a few weeks later. I happily agreed. And that was the moment my trip changed.

Mr. Hiroshi and I spent hours walking and talking about the disaster, how the Japanese people respond in times of crisis and his love for his country. The cherry

Energy-conservation poster in a Tokyo subway station. The 2011 earthquake damaged power plants in Japan, so people all across the country tried to conserve energy by reducing lighting and turning off machines. WINHORSE/ISTOCK.COM

blossoms were starting to bloom, and the city was getting ready for the annual cherry blossom festival—a time to celebrate life and new beginnings.

I continued south to Hiroshima, where the blossoms were in full bloom. There I visited the A-Bomb Dome—one of the only remaining structures after the atomic bomb was dropped on the city in 1945. The people had not forgotten what had happened to them, but the city had moved forward to a better place.

The cherry blossoms were starting to bloom in Tokyo when I returned there a few days later. I went looking for the house that my family had lived in. A group of students helped me with directions and then invited me to a *Hanami*—a cherry-blossom viewing party—later that day. I joined my new friends on blankets under the cherry trees. There were hundreds of other people in the park doing the same thing. This was the first time that they had really come together after the earthquake. People were asking each other if their family and friends were okay and talking about how they felt.

Sipping tea under the cherry trees with a new friend in Tokyo. Many people came out to celebrate the cherry blossoms after the earthquake. JOHANNA WAGSTAFFE

In Japanese culture, the cherry blossoms symbolize the ephemeral nature of life—they last for a very short time, like the short time that we are here. It was a perfect time for everyone to come together and reflect on the exquisite beauty and volatility of life. I knew that the Japanese people would get through this difficult time.

WARNING!

Since we may never be able to accurately predict where and when earthquakes will happen, *earthquake early warning systems* may be the best way to get people to safety before the ground starts shaking. The systems that are already in place in areas that are at high risk for earthquakes have saved many lives.

Earthquake early warning systems rely on the fact that the waves from an earthquake travel at different speeds. The P waves travel much faster than the S waves and surface waves—the ones that do most of the shaking. Sensors can therefore detect the arrival of the P waves first, before the damaging waves arrive.

A green tsunami warning siren in Hawaii.
TRUDYWSIMMONS/DREAMSTIME.COM

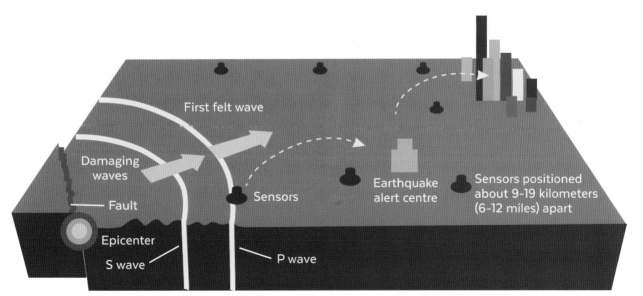

First felt wave

Damaging waves

Fault

Epicenter

S wave

Sensors

Earthquake alert centre

P wave

Sensors positioned about 9-19 kilometers (6-12 miles) apart

An earthquake early warning system relies on sensors to pick up the first waves that an earthquake sends out so that people can be warned before the damaging waves arrive. The farther away you are from the epicenter, the more time you will have. JENN PLAYFORD

QUAKE FACTS

It's not just earthquakes that shake the ground. Underground explosions like nuclear tests also release massive amounts of energy. The seismic waves are picked up by seismometers all over the world, but the seismograms look different from those of earthquakes. Seismology has played a key role in monitoring for nuclear tests by countries like North Korea.

The sensors can calculate where and roughly how big the earthquake is and trigger an alarm if damaging shaking is going to begin. A message center can get this alarm out to city officials, as well as to people's phones and other devices, stating roughly how long they have before the ground starts shaking so they can take cover.

The closer you are to the epicenter of an earthquake, the less time you have between the first waves and the shaking waves. It could be anywhere from a few seconds to a few minutes. But even a few seconds might be enough time to get under a table or a desk and protect yourself from falling objects. It might also be enough time to automatically shut off trains, or stop cars before they cross a bridge or go into a tunnel, or stop a surgeon from starting a delicate procedure. A fifteen-second warning could be enough time to turn off the stove or gather your pets together in a safe place. A sixty-second warning could be enough time for a city to initiate its emergency response plan.

A terrifying image as a massive tsunami rushes through the trees in Thailand following the 2004 Indian Ocean earthquake. DAVID RYDEVIK/WIKIPEDIA.ORG

Children crouch under their desks during an earthquake drill in Japan. By practicing what to do ahead of time, your body will be quicker to react in a real-life situation.
REUTERS/ALAMY STOCK PHOTO

M9.1: INDONESIA, 2004

On December 26, 2004, a megathrust earthquake hit off the west coast of Sumatra, Indonesia, with an estimated magnitude of between 9.0 and 9.3. A result of the Indian Plate sliding under the Burma Plate, the earthquake lifted the ocean floor several meters, triggering a tsunami that smashed into Indian Ocean coastlines hundreds of kilometers away, with waves of up to 30 meters (100 feet). Many tourists were on beaches, enjoying their Christmas holidays, and didn't even know an earthquake had happened until the tsunami arrived. In total, 230,000 people across fourteen countries were killed in one of the deadliest natural disasters in recorded history.

GETTING A HEAD START

Japan is a world leader in earthquake early warning systems. More than 4,300 seismometers have been installed across Japan, and when the first waves of a potentially damaging earthquake are picked up, an alert is sent out to the public through television, radio, the Internet and cell phones. The amount of warning time depends on how far away the receiver is from the earthquake. But even a few seconds' warning can save lives.

Japan also has a network of buoys in the Pacific Ocean that detect tsunamis. If a tsunami is detected, coastal communities will get an alert and the tsunami sirens will go off. People can then follow evacuation routes to get to higher elevation quickly.

In 2011 Chile announced that it would start working on an earthquake early warning system, similar to its own tsunami warning system. When a magnitude 8.3 earthquake struck Chile on a national holiday in 2015, many people at the beach got the earthquake and tsunami warning on their phones so that everyone made it to safety in time.

The us Geological Survey has been working to develop an earthquake early warning system for California, Oregon and Washington since 2006, and California has been working on its own system, called ShakeAlert. British Columbia is also working on a province-wide early warning system.

Since every country has unique geology and fault systems, each country has to do its own research to find out what kind of early warning system will work best. In Mexico, for example, since Mexico City is vulnerable to earthquakes that happen far away, the city can have several minutes of lead time. Other countries, like Turkey, Romania, China, Italy and Taiwan, have developed their own systems, but with varying degrees of success. There is a lot of work still to do.

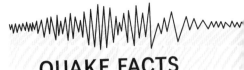

QUAKE FACTS

The US Geological Survey is using real-time reports of shaking on Twitter to help fill gaps in its network of sensors. Maybe social media will be the key to early warning systems in the near future!

Q&A

Q: CAN ANIMALS SENSE EARTHQUAKES BEFORE THEY HAPPEN?

A: People have long believed that animals can predict earthquakes. In ancient Greece, for example, rats and snakes were believed to leave their nests several days before a destructive earthquake. There have also been stories of chickens that stop laying eggs, bees that leave their hives in a panic, and countless cats and dogs acting strangely before an earthquake.

Some animals might be sensitive enough to notice the arrival of the P wave, the first earthquake wave, which humans can't feel, seconds or minutes before the ground starts shaking. As for sensing a quake several days before an earthquake—that is still not well understood. It may be that animals can sense other things that sometimes happen before earthquakes, like changes in groundwater and electrical or magnetic fields, or releases of gases from underground. Lots of scientists are studying animals' sensitivity to these things, but not enough is understood to use it to predict earthquakes.

A collapsed building after the earthquake in Nepal. Nearly 3.5 million people were left homeless. SOMJIN KLONG-UGKARA/ SHUTTERSTOCK.COM

Earthquake survivors in Kathmandu stay sheltered in a camp after the Nepal earthquake.
Many people lost their homes and villages and had nowhere to go. SAŠA PETRICIC/CBC

M7.8: NEPAL, 2015

On April 25, 2015, two continental plates that had been locked together for decades snapped loose. The result was a shallow magnitude 7.8 earthquake in Nepal. A 120-kilometer (75-mile) rupture in the earth's crust ran right through the country's capital, Kathmandu. The shaking resulted in building collapses and landslides, killing over 9,000 people, injuring thousands more and leaving thousands of others homeless. The aftershocks that followed continued to collapse already weakened buildings, many of them World Heritage Sites. The earthquake also triggered avalanches on nearby Mount Everest, killing dozens of climbers and stranding many on the mountain.

ALL TOGETHER NOW

A lot of research on earthquakes is done in universities. But many countries also have a government department dedicated to monitoring and researching earthquakes, and they often make the information from their seismometers available to the public.

In Canada, for example, Geological Survey of Canada is responsible for earthquake monitoring and research. We have hundreds of seismometers across the country that help our seismologists provide information about an earthquake after it happens on its website and on Twitter.

In the United States, the US Geological Survey's Earthquake Hazards Program monitors and reports earthquakes, assesses earthquake impacts and hazards, and researches the causes and effects of earthquakes. There are also hundreds of seismometers across the United States.

The great thing about having a network of thousands of seismometers around the world is that scientists everywhere can use that information in their research on how earthquakes work and how to prepare for them.

An earthquake-research station where seismologists monitor and study earthquake signals from all over the world. MILA SUPINSKAYA GLASHCHENKO/ SHUTTERSTOCK.COM

TOOLS IN THE SKY

We've been talking about tools and technology that are used during earthquakes and sometimes beforehand. But technology is useful afterward as well.

The first twenty-four hours after an earthquake are often the most crucial for saving lives. Seismometers on the ground tell search-and-rescue crews where and how strong an earthquake was. But it's actually technology in the sky that can help them understand where help is needed most.

Satellite and GPS (Global Positioning System) data can be quickly combined to create three-dimensional models of how much ground was displaced after a quake. That information in turn can help first responders get a better idea of how the infrastructure of a city might be damaged and what areas pose the greatest risk to people on the ground during a catastrophe. Satellite images can also help emergency officials figure out quickly if airports and roads have been damaged or if landslides have happened.

Drones are another great new tool for helping people after earthquakes. They can help response teams by getting to areas that would take hours to get to on the ground—in minutes. They can then send back pictures that provide information about how much destruction has happened in remote villages and if there are survivors. These pictures can also be sent to the rest of the world within hours of a natural disaster, so that aid agencies know what is needed and can mobilize fast. Both satellites and drones proved extremely useful after the 2015 Nepal earthquake, when many remote villages in the mountains needed help quickly.

Drones were a critical tool used to identify areas that were hit hard in the Nepal earthquake. This was one of the first times that drones were really utilized to access remote villages that had been cut-off to assess relief needs. DUTOURDUMONDE PHOTOGRAPHY /SHUTTERSTOCK.COM

Susan, NEPAL

The earthquake happened on Saturday. I was at home with my mother, brother and maternal uncle. My father was in Bhaktapur. He is a mechanic who specializes in repairing elevators. We were watching television. First, the electricity was gone. It is normal for the electricity to be cut off in Nepal. But before we could guess if it was the cut-off time, everything started moving—the cupboard, television, walls and even ourselves.

We live on the ground floor. We heard people screaming. My mother and uncle took us out of the house. We were so frightened that we didn't put slippers or shoes on. The ground was moving like a wave. Poles and houses were shaking. Some flower pots from the houses were falling to the ground. An old lady

Volunteers and aid workers from all over the world helped recovery efforts following the Nepal earthquake.
MARGARET EVANS/CBC

beside me fainted. One of my neighbors who lived on the fourth floor was hurt badly while running down the stairs. Everything was like a terrifying dream. It was hard to believe what was going on, why the ground was shaking so fiercely. My mother pulled me and my brother to look for an open space, but our neighborhood is densely populated, so it was hard to find one. We and our neighbors kept running. When we found a big open place, it was already packed with people.

After saving ourselves, we thought of my father. We tried the phone a lot, but the network was congested. We stayed in the open space. I was trying to hear what older people were saying. Some were getting news updates from Facebook. People were calling their families and friends to find out if they were safe. My father finally came. He was worried and in tears. He said that at the time of the earthquake, he was repairing an elevator in the shopping mall. The elevator fell to the ground floor, and he was able to escape it. Luckily, he could run away quickly. Just in front of the mall, a big gate beside the main road fell and trapped three people.

In the evening we got some of our clothes from home and came back to the open space. We had no tents. We slept under a cold open sky that night. The ground was shaking every two to three hours. I was afraid that the ground might tear apart and that we would fall inside it. But thankfully, that never happened.

After a few days we went to our ancestral home in Pokhara. The earthquake epicenter was near Kathmandu, so Pokhara was a bit safer.

Rescue crews search through the rubble for survivors following the Nepal earthquake. JESSICA LINZEY

5

Ready?

Johanna's Story

Learning about the different ways British Columbia is preparing for an earthquake. Here, a member of the Urban Search and Rescue Task Force shows me how teams will cut through different materials to find survivors after an earthquake. JESSICA LINZEY

On December 29, 2015, much of southwestern British Columbia, where I live, got a late-night wake-up call. I had just started to fall asleep, shortly after 11:30 PM, when the dream I was having suddenly involved being rocked from side to side in a boat. I opened my eyes and realized that the rocking wasn't a dream. My husband and I knew that our bed is a safe place to be during an earthquake—there are no pictures or shelves nearby that could fall on us—and it would be dangerous to get up and find something to take cover under. So as the shaking continued, we held on to the side of the bed and waited. I was worried that it might be the beginning of a much larger earthquake. But the shaking stopped after a few seconds.

The power was still on, and my cell phone and computer were still working. I texted the rest of my family to make sure they were okay. Then I checked the seismic station closest to Vancouver, and sure enough, there was the signature of an earthquake. Within minutes, the scientific details were available at both Earthquakes Canada and the US Geological Survey for me to analyze. I began to receive tweets from dozens of people asking questions. Was this a foreshock to a bigger earthquake? Would there be more shaking that night? Was it okay to go back to bed? Should they be getting to higher ground? I answered as best I could: no tsunami was generated, there was a chance of a small aftershock but it was okay to go back to bed, and, because of its location, the earthquake was not likely connected to a bigger main quake.

After the December 2015 earthquake near Victoria, BC, a lot of people wanted to know more about how to prepare themselves for a larger earthquake. Here, on CBC's local evening news in Vancouver, I am discussing the work that still needs to be done. CBC

The CBC called and asked me to go in to work, because it was receiving dozens of calls too from scared people. The evening national News Network show stayed on, live, until 3:00 AM, and then I stayed an hour longer answering questions on social media. We spent much of the next day talking about the earthquake online, on the radio and on television. It was the first time in over ten years that Vancouver and Victoria had experienced an earthquake—and had an actual reminder that we live in a serious earthquake zone.

Like Japan and Chile, Canada and the United States (in the Pacific Northwest) are at risk of having a "big one"—an earthquake of over 9.0 in magnitude that will generate a major tsunami. But it is just as likely that there will be an inland earthquake, a 6.0 or 7.0 magnitude earthquake at a shallow depth. This will still cause a lot of damage, especially in large cities like Vancouver and Seattle, because the epicenter will be closer than it will be in the "big one."

Countries like Japan, Chile and New Zealand get smaller rumbles like this one all the time. As a result, everyone knows what to do when an earthquake happens. The children in the classrooms—just like my kindergarten class in Tokyo—know exactly what to do. The public and the government have constant reminders about how important earthquake safety is, from building codes to earthquake kits to early warning systems, and even just plain understanding what's going on inside the earth.

One thing that many people here in British Columbia said about the earthquake was that it took them a long time to figure out what was happening. They ran out into hallways and streets instead of protecting themselves. The next time an earthquake happens here, I hope people will remember to drop, cover and hold on. And I hope they will not feel as scared, no matter how small or large the earthquake is, because they understand what is happening and have a plan in place.

Blue lines on streets in Wellington, New Zealand, indicate tsunami safe zones that people need to evacuate to. After an earthquake, a tsunami may sweep many kilometers inland. CHAMELEONSEYE/ SHUTTERSTOCK.COM

Many scientists believe that we may never be able to exactly forecast when and where earthquakes will strike. But the more we study what is going on beneath us, the more we will understand how stresses build up between plates. Scientists are already getting better at figuring out which parts of the world are most likely to have damaging earthquakes. And that means better preparation is possible for the people who live in those areas and the buildings they live, work and go to school in.

BE PREPARED, NOT SCARED!

If you live in an area that is prone to earthquakes, there are ways you can prepare yourself. And knowing that you are ready for one will make you feel less frightened.

QUAKE TIP

Practice makes perfect! Ask your family and teachers if you can join millions of people around the world and practice Drop, Cover and Hold On in the annual Great ShakeOut Earthquake Drill. The drill gives people at home, school and work a chance to prepare for earthquakes. You can find out more at www.shakeout.org.

Students at Notre Dame Regional Secondary School in Vancouver, BC, practice getting under their desks in an earthquake drill. CBC

M4.8: BRITISH COLUMBIA, 2015

On December 29, 2015, a magnitude 4.8 earthquake struck just 17 kilometers (10 miles) northeast of Victoria, British Columbia, near Vancouver, at a depth of 52 kilometers (32 miles). It was not a very strong earthquake, but light shaking was felt all across the south coast of British Columbia and the state of Washington. This was what seismologists call a "good" earthquake: no one was hurt and there was no major damage. But it got people to take action. Many got earthquake kits. They talked to their families about an earthquake plan. And they asked questions of scientists, the government and schools.

So are you prepared for when the ground starts shaking? Is your home as safe as it could be if the walls were to start rocking? What kinds of things would you need if the power stayed off for several days or even weeks? And does your whole family know what to do and where to meet after an earthquake?

PREPARE YOURSELF

If you feel the ground start shaking under you, there are just three things you need to do right away:

DROP—COVER—HOLD ON.

DROP to the ground immediately and take COVER by getting under a sturdy desk or table. HOLD ON to it until the shaking stops.

If there isn't something sturdy to get under, cover your face and head with your arms and crouch in a corner of the room you're in. Do not try and run to another room—you have to act quickly, and you might be knocked to the ground. Do not run outside, because you can easily fall or be hit by falling objects.

Experts around the world agree that this is the best way for people to protect themselves during earthquakes.

DON'T PANIC

DROP

COVER

HOLD

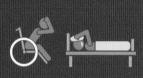

PROTECT YOUR HEAD

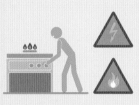

TURN OFF
GAS/ELECTRICITY

EXTINGUISH FIRE

FIND A WAY OUT

STAY AWAY FROM
WINDOWS/ELEVATORS/STAIRS

GO ON HIGHER GROUND

PAY ATTENTION TO ROCKS FALLING

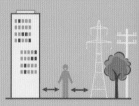

KEEP DISTANCE FROM
BUILDINGS/TREES/POWER LINES

HELP NEIGHBORS

GO TO ASSEMBLY POINT

HELP WITH FIRST AID

STAY INFORMED

If you remember only one thing during an earthquake, it should be to drop, cover and hold on. But have a conversation with your family now to talk about the other important steps to take. ELENABSL/DREAMSTIME.COM

QUAKE TIP

In my own emergency kit, I've also got extra phone chargers, in case there is still electricity and cell phone service, and mini solar panels, in case there is phone service but no electricity.

PREPARE YOUR HOME

After a big earthquake, it is very likely that there will be power outages or water shut-offs. And it may be several days before essential services can be restored. Grocery stores may be closed for a long time. And it may not be safe to travel right away. So you need to have food, water and light where you are to get you through the first few days.

Make sure you have an emergency kit in a place that is easy to get to. Most emergency response organizations recommend that you keep food, water and medication in your kit to last you for at least three days.

An example of an earthquake kit. Can you name all the items? SKODONNELL/ISTOCK.COM

Most injuries that occur during an earthquake are caused by falling or flying objects. Work with your family to secure heavy furniture, like bookcases and dressers, to the wall so they won't fall over. Put breakable and heavy objects down low. You can also buy special earthquake sticky tape to secure objects to a shelf.

You can reduce the risk of injury by keeping your bed away from windows that might break, pictures that might fall or shelves that objects might fall from.

QUAKE TIP

If there are places that have more damage and need attention first, it may take several days for emergency crews to make it to your street. They will make it to your home eventually. In the meantime, listen to the radio for instructions.

Nonperishable food items are a very important part of your emergency kit. Following an earthquake, you may be without power for a long time, so be sure you have food that won't spoil. DARRYL BROOKS/SHUTTERSTOCK.COM

EMERGENCY KIT

Here is a very basic list of what to keep in an emergency kit:

FOOD AND WATER—at least 2 liters (2 quarts) per person per day, and non-perishable food for three days (don't forget pet food!)

RADIO AND FLASHLIGHTS—hand-crank or battery powered (and extra batteries)

HYGIENE AND SANITATION—toothbrush, toothpaste, hand sanitizer, wet wipes, towels, garbage bags

CLOTHING—warm clothing, extra change of clothes, sturdy boots, hat, socks, underwear, blankets

PERSONAL ITEMS—identification, contact information, medication, spare eyeglasses, spare house and car keys, toys for children, cash

SMALL FIRST-AID KIT

COMFORT ITEMS—things that might be comforting in a crisis, like a toy or a family photo album

PREPARE YOUR FAMILY

Every family, no matter how big or small, should have an earthquake plan.

- Decide who will grab the emergency kit, once the shaking stops, and who will take care of gathering your pets.
- Know how to get out of your home safely after the shaking stops. If you live in a high-rise, you'll have to take the stairs, not the elevator.
- Pick three safe places where your family can meet up in case you are not at home when an earthquake happens—one near your home, one in the neighborhood and one near work or school. This will mean much less confusion if cell phones are not working.
- Choose an emergency contact—someone who doesn't live nearby and who can coordinate checking that everyone is safe.

Once your family is all together, the best place to be is probably in your own neighborhood. You will know the people there, and you will come together as a community to get through the first few days. If your home has no obvious damage or cracks in the foundation or walls, you can probably stay inside. But many people choose to camp out on their streets, at their local school or in a park after an earthquake, not just out of concern about aftershocks but also because being part of a group of people after a disaster can be much more comforting.

QUAKE TIP

Another thing you can do to prepare for an earthquake is take a first-aid course, so that you can help injured people after an earthquake.

Water will be needed not only for drinking, but for washing, cleaning and cooking as well.
SERGEY RYZHOV/SHUTTERSTOCK.COM

After an earthquake many people will stay in makeshift communities, often in public spaces like parks. This camp was at a park in Nepal following the 2015 earthquake. DUTOURDUMONDE PHOTOGRAPHY/SHUTTERSTOCK.COM

AND REMEMBER...

Every part of the world has unique risks. Depending on where you live, you may have to plan for tornadoes or blizzards or hurricanes. Understanding the science behind the processes of this active planet that we live on, and knowing what to do if disaster strikes, will make you feel more safe.

The earthquake-education exhibit at the natural history museum in San Francisco, CA. The earth is a complicated, at times dangerous and active planet! But it's the best one we've got, so let's try to understand and respect it the best we can.
ANTON_IVANOV/SHUTTERSTOCK.COM

Freya Johansen, VANCOUVER

Seven -year -old Freya Johansen knows exactly what to do during an earthquake, and that makes her less scared about them. KENT JOHANSEN

Johanna: Tell me about the night your parents woke you up before the earthquake.

Freya: I was lying in my bed, fast asleep. See this teddy bear? Pretend this is me. I was sleeping just like this [she pretends to make the teddy bear snore]. All of a sudden my parents were in my bedroom, shaking me awake. My mom pulled the covers off me! She told me to follow them under the table. Right then the room started shaking! A picture that I had painted fell over on a shelf. And then my fairy princess dolls started to fall over.

Johanna: What happened while you were under the table?

Freya: Well, it was me, my mom, my dad and my dog. We held on to the table legs until the shaking stopped, and then we stayed under there for a little while longer.

Johanna: Were you scared?

Freya: No, not really.

Johanna: What if it had been a larger earthquake?

Freya: Like more shaking with aftershocks? Then this would have happened. [She demonstrates a larger earthquake by shaking her bedside table until everything that was on it has fallen off onto the floor, including a plant. I look around to make sure we're not going to get in trouble for this]. Well, then I should probably make sure there's not so much stuff near me that can fall on me.

QUAKE FACTS

If a boat is out at sea when an earthquake hits under the ocean, there is actually very little effect on the ship by the earthquake itself. Even if a tsunami is generated, in the deeper waters the tsunami is more like a large swell, since there is more room for the water to spread out. But if the boat is closer to port, where the tsunami wave grows larger in height, it will feel the full force of the waves as they head inland. Often there is enough time between an earthquake and a tsunami for boats close to port to head out into the open ocean and away from danger.

Freya playing with her toys on a boat. KENT JOHANSEN

Acknowledgments

FIRST, A BIG THANK-YOU TO MY FAMILY. Whether for running, reading, quoting, making tea or making a joke—I keep needing you. And thank you, Mama, for letting me share a small piece of your incredible journey through life with Papa.

To Esra, Ria, Hiroko, Susan, Kent and Freya: thank you for reliving such traumatic experiences and sharing your stories with other children around the world. Thanks to Vanessa, for connecting me with Esra and for your advice, over wine, early on, and to Lena and the whole team from Global Buddy Schools, for your great work with children after the Nepal earthquake and for allowing me to share a story.

So many wonderful connections were made in finding a story of the Japanese earthquake to share. Mike Tanaka, Beatrix Yoshikawa, Graham Chave, Christian Hansen and Sean Mahoney: thank you for your help and guidance along the way. And thank you to Hiroshi Tanoue, who continues to make my love for Japan grow.

A special thank-you to Dr. Hannah Bentham, for all of your seismo and general life guidance! And to our original seismic god, DE, who brought us together.

I would also like to acknowledge the significant support from the CBC and my colleagues over the years in allowing me to develop my science reporting skills. The opportunities I've had to try new ways to educate and inform Canadians have continued to make my job an exciting one.

Many thanks to the whole team at Orca Book Publishers. The process has been a new one for me, but right from the start Ruth Linka has been a great mentor. Thanks to Merrie-Ellen Wilcox for working her magic; I truly understand the importance of a good editor now! And thank you, Jenn Playford, for taking the whole book to the next level with your beautiful illustrations and layout. I want them all framed! I feel very proud to be a small part of such a great Canadian publishing company.

And last but not least, to my husband, Tristan—thank you for understanding me the best.

A replica of the Statue of Liberty, surrounded by tsunami destruction, stands tall in Ishinomaki, Japan, following the 2011 earthquake.
ENASE/ISTOCK.COM

Resources

WEBSITES

CBC Vancouver earthquake podcast 'Fault Lines':
www.cbc.ca/radio/podcasts/fault-lines/

Discovering Geology, British Geological Survey:
www.bgs.ac.uk/discoveringGeology/hazards/earthquakes/home.html

Earthquake Hazards Program, United States Geological Survey:
http://earthquake.usgs.gov/earthquakes

Earthquakes Canada, Geological Survey of Canada:
www.earthquakescanada.nrcan.gc.ca

Earthquakes for Kids, United States Geological Survey:
http://earthquake.usgs.gov/learn/kids

Great ShakeOut: www.shakeout.org

Latest Earthquakes: http://earthquake.usgs.gov/earthquakes/map

Ready for Earthquakes: www.ready.gov/earthquakes

Ready for Tsunamis: www.ready.gov/tsunamis

Seismograms from around the world: https://earthquake.usgs.gov
monitoring/operations/network.php?virtual_network=GSN

VIDEOS

An Illustrated Guide to Reading a Seismogram:
www.usgs.gov/media/videos/illustrated-guide-reading-seismogram

How Tsunamis Work (TED-Ed):
https://www.youtube.com/watch?v=Wx9vPv-T51I

Tsunamis: Know What to Do!:
www.youtube.com/watch?v=UzR0Rt3i4kc

Glossary

aftershock—a smaller earthquake that happens after the main quake, as the earth settles into its new position

body waves—seismic waves that travel through the interior of the earth during an earthquake

building code—a set of rules made by a government for how buildings must be designed, constructed and repaired

continental collision—the name used when two continental plates push into each other

convection—a process in which magma rises from the earth's core to its crust, then cools and sinks again, keeping the surface in constant motion

convergent boundary—the type of boundary formed when two tectonic plates collide

core—the scorching center of the earth, which includes two layers: the solid inner core and liquid outer core

core sample—a small sample of earth, usually drilled from below the surface

crust—the earth's outer layer

divergent boundary—the type of boundary formed when two tectonic plates move away from each other, usually in the middle of an ocean

drawback—the name for when water is pulled back from the shoreline during a tsunami; one of the warning signs that a large wave is coming

earthquake—shaking of the ground when seismic energy is released by a sudden movement in a fault

earthquake early warning system—a system of sensors that can detect the earliest seismic waves and warn people that an earthquake is coming

earthquake zones—regions of the world where seismic activity and earthquakes are more frequent. Usually situated near fault lines.

epicenter—the point on the earth's surface directly above the hypocenter, where energy is released during an earthquake

fault—a crack in the earth

foreshock—an earthquake that happens before a larger earthquake

geography—a science that deals with the diverse physical, biological and cultural features of the earth's surface

humanitarian aid—the aid and action designed to save lives, alleviate suffering and maintain and protect human dignity during and in the aftermath of man-made crises and natural disasters

hypocenter—the exact point where energy is released within the earth during an earthquake

lava—magma that breaks through the earth's surface

liquefaction—the name for when the shaking from an earthquake turns solid soil into a kind of mud that makes the shaking stronger

logarithmic scale—the kind of scale used to measure earthquakes, where each number on the scale is the previous amount multiplied by another amount

magma—hot liquid rock

magnitude—a number that represents the relative size of an earthquake

mantle—the middle layer of the earth, between the core and the surface

megathrust—a magnitude 9.0 earthquake that can happen in subduction zones

meteorologist—a scientist who studies the atmosphere

meteorology—the study of the atmosphere, including climate and weather

moment magnitude scale—a scale that can measure the size of earthquakes in terms of the energy released; the most accurate scale for earthquakes greater than magnitude 8.0

oceanic crust—the top layer of an oceanic plate

primary wave (P wave)—the first seismic wave to reach the earth's surface during an earthquake

Richter scale—one of the first widely used methods of measuring earthquakes; not very accurate for large earthquakes

Ring of Fire—the large area along the fringes of the Pacific Plate (the tectonic plate covering almost the entire floor of the Pacific Ocean) in which most earthquakes and volcanoes occur

rupture zone—the section of the earth that releases stress during an earthquake

secondary wave (S wave)—the second seismic wave to reach the earth's surface during an earthquake

seismic waves—the energy that is sent out from the hypocenter during an earthquake

seismogram—the image created by a seismometer that seismologists read to get information about earthquakes

seismologist—a scientist who studies earthquakes and seismic waves

seismology—the study of earthquakes and seismic waves

seismometer—a sensitive detector that picks up seismic waves traveling through the earth

subduction zone—the type of zone where an ocean plate collides with a continental plate, and where earthquakes greater than magnitude 9.0 can happen

surface waves—seismic waves that travel along the earth's surface and cause most of the damage during an earthquake

tectonic plates—pieces of the earth's crust that fit together and are constantly shifting because of convection below

TNT (trinitrotoluene)—a very powerful explosive

transform boundary—the type of boundary formed when two tectonic plates slide past each other

tsunami—a series of large and fast-moving waves caused by an earthquake that happens under an ocean

Index

*Page numbers in **bold** indicate an image; there may also be text related to the same topic on that page*

Index (continued)